Eleven Acronyms
Every Pilot Should Know

By

Mark Pierce

Library of Congress Control Number: 2026902659
ISBN: 979-8-218-92685-4
First Edition
Pierce Aviation Press
Printed in the United States of America

Disclaimer:
This book is an independent educational resource and is not an official publication of the Federal Aviation Administration (FAA). While the acronyms and mnemonics discussed here are commonly taught in FAA training materials and widely used in primary flight instruction, this book has not been reviewed, endorsed, or approved by the FAA. It is intended to support aspiring pilots in understanding and applying these concepts, but readers should always refer to current FAA regulations, advisory circulars, and official guidance for authoritative information.

Additionally, the views expressed are those of the author and do not reflect the official guidance or position of the United States Government, the Department of Defense or of the United States Air Force.

Dedication

To all student pilots who pursue the skies with courage and curiosity.

And to my brothers and sisters in the United States Air Force — and across all branches of service — whose tradition of excellence continues to inspire me. May you, too, one day "slip the surly bonds of Earth" with confidence, discipline, and joy.

Acknowledgments

I would like to acknowledge my wife of more than forty years, Lourdes. She has been my greatest supporter in the pursuit of my dream to fly.

I am also deeply grateful to Beth Stanton, Editor, *Mentor* magazine, for contributing the foreword to this book and for lending her wisdom and perspective as a pilot to its opening pages.

Foreword

Learning how to fly involves a bewildering amount of information. You quickly discover that aviation loves acronyms. It can feel like alphabet soup: IMSAFE, PAVE, ARROW, etc. You memorize them, repeat them on demand, and sometimes wonder whether they'll actually help when things get busy in the cockpit.

This book is here to answer that question with a confident yes.

What Mark Pierce has done is take the acronyms every pilot encounters and put them in context. Instead of treating them as memory tricks to be recited and forgotten, he connects each one to the decisions pilots make before and during flight. They are practical tools grounded in FAA guidance, the Airman Certification Standards, and years of instructional experience, all aimed at helping pilots think clearly, manage risk, and make better choices.

As you move through these pages, you'll notice a deliberate progression. Each acronym builds on the next. He shows how these tools fit together, where they come from, and how they support real-world decision-making. These are the same concepts instructors teach, examiners expect, and pilots rely on every day — presented here in an approachable, logical, and practical way.

Whether you're a student pilot feeling overwhelmed, a certificated pilot brushing up for a flight review, or an instructor looking for a better way to explain the "why" behind the rules, this book will feel familiar and useful.

It doesn't replace official FAA publications, and it doesn't try to. Instead, it will help you connect and apply the information in them with enhanced understanding.

If this book helps you move beyond rote memorization and toward disciplined, thoughtful flying, it will have done exactly what it set out to do.

Beth Stanton
Director of Publications and Editor
National Association of Flight Instructors

Preface

Thank you for purchasing this book. My intent in writing it is to introduce aspiring pilots to what can at times feel like an overwhelming amount of material. By breaking down the acronyms most commonly used in pilot training — and explaining the FAA guidance behind many of them — student pilots can develop a practical framework to enhance their studies.

The goal is to go beyond rote memorization and reveal the underlying sources behind each acronym. In doing so, readers will be introduced to foundational documents such as FAA Handbooks, Advisory Circulars (ACs), Federal Aviation Regulations (FARs), and the Airman Certification Standards (ACS). These references form the knowledge base required of every Pilot in Command (PIC).

I encourage readers to become familiar with these source materials. A simple search of the references mentioned here can open the door to deeper study and a stronger frame of reference. In fact, while doing research for this book, I discovered new insights — evidence that even experienced aviators benefit from revisiting the basics.

My hope is that this book serves as a useful companion for aspiring, novice, intermediate, and seasoned general aviation pilots alike, helping each to build confidence, strengthen decision-making, and fly with greater safety and understanding.

Table of Contents

Introduction

At first, the path to becoming a pilot seems daunting. Understanding the concepts of flight, new terms particular to aviation, and Federal Aviation Regulations (FARs) can be intimidating even to the most motivated aspiring pilot. The intent of this book is to focus on common acronyms. In each case, the book breaks down the acronym and links it back to the source requirement or relevant application to Single-Pilot Resource Management (SRM). In doing so, the book goes beyond rote memory to understanding, application, and ultimately correlation.

To set the stage for the book, it is important to define Single-Pilot Resource Management. According to the Federal Aviation Administration (FAA) FAA-H-8083-2A *Risk Management Handbook* (June 2022), Single-Pilot Resource Management is defined as:

> Single-Pilot resource management (SRM) specifically refers to appropriate management of all resources available to the single pilot. SRM includes competencies such as situational awareness, communication skills, teamwork, task allocation, aeronautical decision-making, risk management, controlled flight into terrain (CFIT) awareness, and automation management. Resources are found both inside and outside the aircraft.

From this SRM definition, the acronyms represented in this book directly focus on two competencies of SRM – Aeronautical Decision Making (ADM) and Risk

Management. Since the focus is on these two competencies, here is the definition of each.

FAA Advisory Circular (AC) 60-22 *Aeronautical Decision Making* dated December 13, 1991, defines ADM as:

> ADM is a systematic approach to the mental process used by aircraft pilots to consistently determine the best course of action in response to a given set of circumstances.

The *Risk Management Handbook* (FAA-H-8083-2A) defines Risk Management as:

> The part of the decision-making process which relies on situational awareness, problem recognition, and good judgment to reduce risks associated with each flight.

AC 60-22 also codified DECIDE (**D**etect, **E**stimate, **C**hoose, **I**dentify, **D**o, **E**valuate), one of the acronyms of this book. While it has been over 30 years since the FAA defined ADM and codified DECIDE, the ADM concept and the DECIDE method of application are still extremely relevant today. In fact, the FAA's emphasis on ADM is further developed through the FAA Safety Team's (FAASTeam[1]) introduction of the 3P model—**P**erceive, **P**rocess, **P**erform—around 2005. In doing so, the FAA shifted from a reactive DECIDE

[1] FAASTeam is the educational outreach arm of the FAA, the FAASTeam supports initiatives like the WINGS Pilot Proficiency Program, aviation maintenance training, and UAS safety education.

model to a simpler 3P proactive model, both of which are still taught.

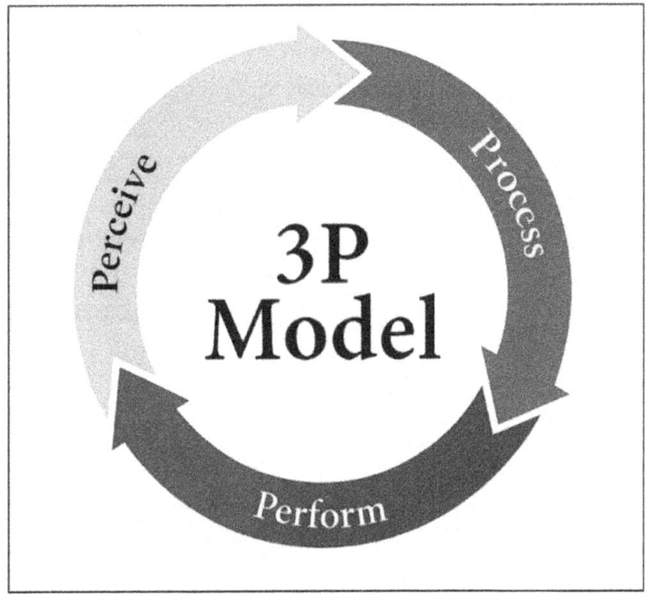

Figure 1 – The 3P Model

The shift to the proactive 3P model provides a starting point for subsequent acronyms since using the 3P model sets the stage for PAVE, CARE, and TEAM, each of which can be used in the Perceive, Process, and Perform steps of the 3P model. In deciding how to order the acronyms for this book, it was important to give context to the acronyms. Therefore, the book starts with the 3P model and steps through PAVE, CARE, and TEAM as they represent Perceive, Process, and Perform, respectively. Next, the book walks through the sub parts of PAVE, namely IMSAFE, ARROW, AV1ATES, A TOMATO FLAMES, FLAPS, and

NWKRAFT. The book finishes by exploring the DECIDE model since it has foundational insights into the decision-making process.

While most PICs do not consciously think they are starting with Perceive, Process, and Perform, each flight attempted likely uses some form of the 3P model. It is equally important to emphasize the acronyms are intertwined. Often starting with one acronym leads to referencing another to complete the effort of the first acronym. This will seem overwhelming at first, however, the intent of the book is to put each acronym in context for the task at hand and provide a logical method to better utilize each acronym. Furthermore, the effort of putting each acronym in context provides the linkage to various FARs, ACs, and the Airman Certification Standards. In each case, the supporting documentation will be clearly identified for further exploration, elevating the acronyms from rote to understanding, application, and correlation.

A final note on the relationship of acronyms to mnemonics. An acronym is a word formed from the initial letters of a phrase, such as ARROW for required aircraft documents. A mnemonic is a memory aid, a tool designed to help recall information more easily. In aviation training, acronyms often function as mnemonics because they condense complex requirements or procedures into simple, memorable cues. While not all acronyms are mnemonics, in practice the two terms overlap: acronyms become mnemonics when they serve as mental shortcuts that reinforce learning and aid recall during flight preparation or decision-making. By treating acronyms as mnemonics, student pilots move beyond rote memorization and begin to see them as tools for safer, more disciplined flying.

Chapter 1: 3P – Perceive, Process, Perform

Before diving into the 3P model, it is essential to set the context of two key terms: Risk and Hazard. The Federal Aviation Administration's (FAA) 2022 *Risk Management Handbook* (FAA-H-8083-2A) starts out chapter 3 with a discussion on the relationship of Risk and Hazard. In fact, the handbook readily recognizes the two words can easily be confused and uses Title 14 of the Code of Federal Regulations (CFR) to define each term. Per 14 CFR § 5.3, Definitions, "Hazard" and "Risk" are defined as:

> Hazard means a condition or an object that could foreseeably cause or contribute to an incident or aircraft accident, as defined in 49 CFR § 830.2.
>
> Risk means the composite of predicted severity and likelihood of the potential effect of a hazard.

The value of the Risk Management Handbook is that it simplifies the relationship between Hazard and Risk with the following summary:

> Simply put, a hazard is a condition that could cause an accident. The probability and predicted severity of the consequences that may result from any hazard is the risk. Identifying, analyzing, and responding appropriately to hazards decreases the risks and increases the margin of safety.

To simplify it even further, imagine a banana peel on a sidewalk. The banana peel itself is the hazard—a condition that could cause harm. The risk is the probability of slipping on it and the potential severity of the injury if you do. In other words, we perceive the hazard, then process the risk associated with it.

With the relationship between hazard and risk appropriately put into perspective, the 3P model can be explored in the context of risk mitigation to any identified hazards. Broken down into its simplest form, the 3P model consists of the following:

1. **Perceive** the given set of circumstances.
2. **Process** by evaluating their impact on flight safety.
3. **Perform** by implementing the best course of action.

In short, a PIC must be able to react to situations and logically determine the best solution. But how? 3P can be put into two categories – preflight planning and inflight execution. For preflight planning consider the following steps as part of Aeronautical Decision Making (ADM) and Risk Management.

Step 1 – Perceive to ***identify hazards*** associated with the flight. For this, a PIC might use the PAVE acronym which focuses on four independent items (**P**ilot, **A**ircraft, en**V**ironment, and **E**xternal pressures).

Step 2 – Process to ***assess*** the level of risk each identified hazard presents to the flight. For this, a PIC might use the CARE acronym, which helps evaluate the risk associated with each hazard by examining four independent factors (**C**onsequences, **A**lternatives, **R**eality, and **E**xternal pressures).

Step 3 – Perform to ***mitigate*** the risk by taking the best course of action. For this, a PIC might use the TEAM acronym which focuses on four methods to address the risk (**T**ransfer, **E**liminate, **A**ccept, and **M**itigate).

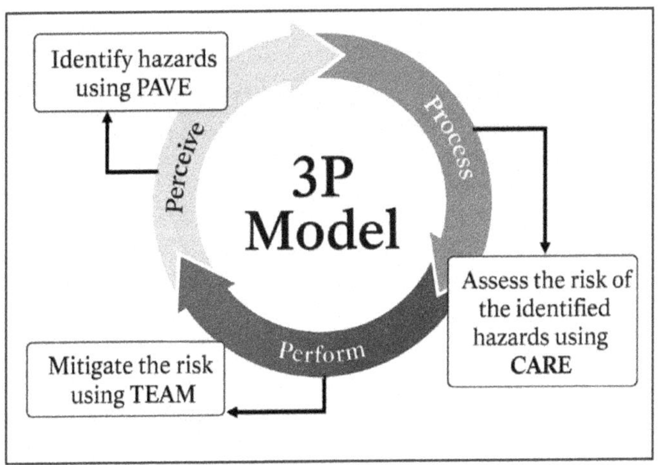

Figure 2. The 3P Model Correlated to Risk Management in the ACS

Relating the 3P model – perceive, process, and perform to identify, assess, and mitigate clearly aligns with the FAA's Private Pilot for Airplane Category Airman Certification Standards (FAA-S-ACS-6C, Dated November 2023) where in every task the criteria for Risk Management states "The applicant is able to identify, assess, and mitigate risk associated with…". To reiterate, using PAVE focuses on the preflight planning process to identify hazards then assess and mitigate the risks associated with the flight before ever getting into the airplane. Clear examples of preflight planning applying the 3P model using acronyms are covered in each of the applicable chapters, but equally important, the FAA focuses on and assesses an applicant pilot's Risk Management through the Airman Certification Standards (ACS) in every task. Therefore, using the 3P model during preflight planning, ground operations, and in-flight execution should become second nature.

For the subsequent example to make more sense, reference the figures 3a, b, and c below. FAA-S-ACS-6C is the private pilot practical test standard. In other words, the ACS is the practical exam broken down into twelve areas of operation (outlined in roman numerals) from preflight preparation to post flight procedures. The Area of Operation X (Multiengine Operations) is not part of the Private Pilot practical exam unless the applicant is pursuing a multiengine rating. Additionally, Area of Operation XI (Night Operations) is not part of the practical exam, rather the training is verified via the applicant's logbook. There is accommodation for pilots training in Alaska where according to 14 CFR § 61.110, an applicant unable to accomplish night training, that applicant, upon passing, will be issued a pilot certificate with a limitation "Night flying prohibited" until that pilot receives the night training (within the subsequent 12-calendar months).

In the ACS, each Area of Operation is broken down into subparts consisting of "Tasks". Each task is broken down further starting with the applicable references, objective, and notes (if applicable) for the task. The references are a good source for information relating to the specific task, although the reference is not specific to the task so it will be up to the applicant to review the reference with respect to the task at hand. The objective defines the specifics for the area of operation in terms of "knowledge, risk management, and skills" for the task. This is key, because the task is further broken down into specific requirements for knowledge, risk management, and skills that make up the objective.

As an example, in the ACS (FAA-S-ACS-6C), Area of Operation IV; Takeoffs, Landings, and Go-Arounds, Task B: Normal Approach and Landing Objective is (see figure 3a):

> To determine the applicant exhibits satisfactory knowledge, risk management, and skills associated with normal approach and landing with emphasis on proper use and coordination of flight controls.

Figure 3. ACS Area of Operation IV. Takeoffs, Landings, and Go-Arounds: Task B. Normal Approach and Landing.

Figure 3a – ACS Area of Operation IV. Takeoffs, Landings, and Go-Arounds: Task B. Normal Approach and Landing–References, Objective, and Knowledge.

Area of Operation IV. Takeoffs, Landings, and Go-Arounds

Task B. Normal Approach and Landing

References: AIM; FAA-H-8083-2, FAA-H-8083-3, FAA-H-8083-23, FAA-H-8083-25; POH/AFM

Objective: To determine the applicant exhibits satisfactory knowledge, risk management, and skills associated with normal approach and landing with emphasis on proper use and coordination of flight controls.

Note: If a crosswind condition does not exist, the applicant's knowledge of crosswind elements must be evaluated through oral testing.

Knowledge: The applicant demonstrates understanding of:

PA.IV.B.K1: A stabilized approach, including energy management concepts.

PA.IV.B.K2: Effects of atmospheric conditions, including wind, on approach and landing performance.

PA.IV.B.K3: Wind correction techniques on approach and landing.

Applying the 3P model to the execution of one of the outlined skills (PA.IV.B.S8, see figure 3c) for the task to "Maintain directional control and appropriate crosswind correction throughout the approach and landing". In-flight, an applicant perceives a crosswind component by assessing the drift on final. The applicant demonstrates knowledge and understanding of "Effects of atmospheric conditions, including wind, on approach and landing performance" (PA.IV.B.K2, see figure 3a). The applicant then processes the effect of the crosswind such that if nothing changes, the safety of the flight and/or the ability to meet the outlined skill is in question. Therefore, the applicant performs a crosswind correction skill (PA.IV.B.S8, see figure 3c) to once again align the aircraft on the runway center/landing path. The result is a demonstration of Risk Management through identifying (perceiving), assessing (processing), and mitigating (performing) the Effects of Crosswind (PA.IV.B.R2a, see figure 3b) for the Flight Examiner.

Figure 3b – ACS Area of Operation IV. Takeoffs, Landings, and Go-Arounds: Task B. Normal Approach and Landing–Risk Management.

Risk
Management: The applicant is able to identify, assess, and mitigate risk associated with:

PA.IV.B.R1: Selection of runway/landing surface, approach path, and touchdown area based on pilot capability, aircraft performance and limitations, available distance, and wind.

PA.IV.B.R2: Effects of:

PA.IV.B.R2a: a. Crosswind

PA.IV.B.R2b: b. Windshear

PA.IV.B.R2c: c. Tailwind

PA.IV.B.R2d: d. Wake turbulence

PA.IV.B.R2e: e. Landing surface/condition

PA.IV.B.R3: Planning for:

PA.IV.B.R3a: a. Rejected landing and go-around

PA.IV.B.R3b: b. Land and hold short operations (LAHSO)

PA.IV.B.R4: Collision hazards.

PA.IV.B.R5: Low altitude maneuvering, including stall, spin, or controlled flight into terrain (CFIT).

PA.IV.B.R6: Distractions, task prioritization, loss of situational awareness, or disorientation.

Throughout training, pilots learn to continuously and subconsciously use the 3P model. They are always looking, through crosschecks, to perceive (or identify) slight changes to expected norms or actions. Once perceived, they are processing (or assessing) the risk of the change and then performing (or mitigating) the risk.

Figure 3c – ACS Area of Operation IV. Takeoffs, Landings, and Go-Arounds: Task B. Normal Approach and Landing–Skills.

Skills: The applicant exhibits the skill to:

PA.IV.B.S1: Complete the appropriate checklist(s).

PA.IV.B.S2: Make radio calls as appropriate.

PA.IV.B.S3: Ensure the airplane is aligned with the correct/assigned runway or landing surface.

PA.IV.B.S4: Scan the runway or landing surface and adjoining area for traffic and obstructions.

PA.IV.B.S5: Select and aim for a suitable touchdown point considering the wind conditions, landing surface, and obstructions.

PA.IV.B.S6: Establish the recommended approach and landing configuration, airspeed, and trim, and adjust pitch attitude and power as required to maintain a stabilized approach.

PA.IV.B.S7: Maintain manufacturer's published approach airspeed or in its absence not more than 1.3 times the stalling speed or the minimum steady flight speed in the landing configuration (VSO), +10/-5 knots with gust factor applied.

PA.IV.B.S8: Maintain directional control and appropriate crosswind correction throughout the approach and landing.

PA.IV.B.S9: Make smooth, timely, and correct control application during round out and touchdown.

PA.IV.B.S10: Touch down at a proper pitch attitude, within 400 feet beyond or on the specified point, with no side drift, and with the airplane's longitudinal axis aligned with and over the runway center/landing path.

PA.IV.B.S11: Execute a timely go-around if the approach cannot be made within the tolerances specified above or for any other condition that may result in an unsafe approach or landing.

PA.IV.B.S12: Use runway incursion avoidance procedures, if applicable.

Other times, using the 3P model may be more overt where there is a deliberate movement through the 3P model. For example, the effects of a change in weather at a destination may trigger a PIC to consciously work through the steps. Enroute, the pilot contacts flight service for a destination weather update which reveals the destination weather is no longer Visual Flight Rules

(VFR). The pilot has perceived/identified a hazard. The PIC then processes/assesses that continuation to the destination airport would be a risk to the flight (potential accident). The pilot then performs/mitigates the risk by executing a change of destination to a preplanned alternate airport.

In summary, focusing on the 3P model first builds a foundation for subsequent acronyms by defining the concepts of hazard and risk and how they are applicable to Aeronautical Decision Making (ADM) and Risk Management. Furthermore, the chapter provided context for the use of 3P by defining the model to set the stage for preflight planning acronyms as well as providing examples of using 3P in-flight. Finally, this chapter identified its direct linkage to the Airman Certification Standards which all general aviation pilots are evaluated as part of their practical flight exam.

Chapter 2: PAVE

This chapter introduces PAVE at the conceptual level. The sub-acronyms that support each element of PAVE — such as IMSAFE for Pilot and ARROW/AV1ATES for Aircraft — will be explored in later chapters. For now, the goal is to understand PAVE as the "Perceive" or "identify" step of the 3P model.

Preflight planning risk mitigation starts with the PAVE acronym. PAVE can be considered the first "P" of Perceive, Process, and Perform model as part of the preflight planning process – Perceive to identify hazards. This one acronym, PAVE, captures four independent hazard elements. It serves as a "roadmap" for many of the subsequent acronyms. The four independent contributors are:

- **P**ilot
- **A**ircraft
- en**V**ironment
- **E**xternal pressures

Starting with the pilot, 14 CFR Part 61 outlines the regulatory requirements for the certification of pilots, flight instructors, and ground instructors in the United States. It specifies eligibility criteria, training and experience requirements, testing procedures, and privileges and limitations associated with various airman certificates, including student, private, commercial, and airline transport pilot licenses. So, for the purposes of simplifying the P in PAVE, assume the student pilot has met the eligibility requirements of 14 CFR Part 61, Subpart C – Student Pilots § 61.83 and has a student pilot certificate. The entirety of 14 CFR Part 61 is not the focus of the P in PAVE, rather Part 61 is listed here as the source for pilot certificate regulatory requirements. Thus, what should preflight planning focus on with respect to the Pilot in PAVE?

The P in PAVE serves to alert the Pilot to identify potential hazards to the flight that might become apparent in a self-evaluation. The acronym IMSAFE (**I**llness, **M**edication, **S**tress, **A**lcohol, **F**atigue, **E**motion described in a subsequent chapter) is used for self-evaluation, however the P is more than a self-evaluation. For example, this is the time for the pilot to ensure the recency of flight is met in accordance with 14 CFR § 61.57. Often a Designated Flight Examiner (DPE) might bring up the concept of current vs. legal in the oral portion of the practical exam with a hypothetical scenario where a pilot is "legal" to fly but might not be as current as the scenario warrants. In this case, the DPE is assessing the applicant's understanding of the legal vs. current concept. While there may be no right or wrong answer, the DPE may be assessing the applicant's ability to identify a potential hazard and what steps the applicant might take to mitigate the risk associated with the hazard thus evaluating the perspective pilot's Aeronautical Decision Making. Let's examine the scenario a bit further.

You recently received your Private Pilot Certificate. You have built up about 20 hours in the last 90 days in the flying club, giving you about 80 hours total time of which about half is PIC time and the other half is dual received time during your private pilot training. You are current for nights, but your last 3 night takeoffs and landings to full stops were over 2 months ago. The flying club aircraft have been hard to schedule, but you promised your good friend who will be visiting you the following week you would take her for a flight. The only time you could schedule the aircraft was an hour after sunset the following week while your friend was in town. While you may be legal to fly your friend, can you identify the hazard(s) in this scenario? What might be the assessed risk of the identified hazard(s)? Would you schedule and fly if you could not mitigate the risks?

Again, there may be no right or wrong answer since you would be legal to fly your friend. However, you might suggest to the DPE that to mitigate the identified hazard, you might schedule a solo night flight or a night flight with a flight instructor before your friend's scheduled flight to elevate your recency of night experience. Flying at night with an instructor or solo after a couple of months of not flying at night at this stage of flight experience shows good ADM, since it mitigates the hazard and reduces the risk associated with flying your friend.

The preceding scenario was meant to elevate the "P" in PAVE representing "Pilot" to more than just the IMSAFE acronym. While an important acronym, IMSAFE may be just a starting point for the self-assessment before each flight. Each pilot must do an objective self-assessment as part of the preflight planning to ensure all hazards have been addressed and where applicable mitigated. As a pilot gains experience, P is an area where complacency can become a hazard in and of itself. That could be part of the FAA's focus on pilots as part of the PAVE acronym.

The "A" in PAVE represents the aircraft, the second hazard element of PAVE. It serves to remind the Pilot In Command (PIC) there are aircraft requirements according to 14 CFR Part 91 which are applicable to every flight. The A in PAVE has many different paths depending on the context for which the PIC assesses the aircraft. Therefore, there are four applicable acronyms associated with the A in PAVE. The first is ARROW which is used to ensure the aircraft has the proper documentation on board and specific weight and balance data is available so the PIC can calculate the takeoff and landing data for the flight. Next, AV1ATES is used to ensure the proper inspections have been accomplished prior to flight. The third is A TOMATO FLAMES which assures the PIC the aircraft has the proper equipment and instruments on board for Visual Flight Rule (VFR) operation. Finally, FLAPS is paired with A TOMATO FLAMES regarding equipment and instrument requirements, except it applies to VFR operation at night. Each of these acronyms associated with the A of PAVE have their own subsequent chapter.

At this point in the preflight planning, suffice to say A in PAVE draws attention to the aircraft. The FAA is particular and directive about documentation, inspections, and equipment needed to ensure the aircraft is safe to operate. Required documentation is covered in 14 CFR § 91.203 for airworthiness and registration and 14 CFR § 91.9 for operating limitations. Inspections are covered in 14 CFR § 91.171, § 91.207, § 91.403, § 91.409, § 91.411. Finally, equipment is covered in 14 CFR § 91.205. Each of these references is a place to start. Specific subsections will be covered in additional detail when exploring the four acronyms associated with the aircraft. As you can imagine, each acronym path of the A of PAVE represents the myriad aspects of ensuring the aircraft is safe to operate.

The V in PAVE is a bit of a misnomer since it refers to the en**V**ironment. Environment is a catchall that deserves consideration by every PIC on every flight. The source of the catchall is 14 CFR § 91.103 – Preflight Action. Fortunately, there is an acronym for that – NWKRAFT or **N**OTAM[2]s, **W**eather, **K**nown traffic delays, **R**unways, **A**lternates, **F**uel, and **T**akeoff and landing data. Each flight is different in that the environment for each flight can change based on many factors. On a typical flight around your local aerodrome, you may only be concerned with the local weather, NOTAMs, and Takeoff and landing data. But introduce a cross-country flight or even a flight to an airport less than 25 nautical miles away and additional preflight actions come into play.

The building block approach in primary flight training towards a private pilot certificate starts with the local airport environment (weather, runway(s), and NOTAMs) plus the aircraft fuel and takeoff and landing data. As the cross-country gets introduced, expanded weather, NOTAMs, known traffic delays, fuel reserves, runways at potential other landing airports and airports

[2] NOTAMs are time-critical notices that alert pilots to temporary conditions or changes affecting flight operations.

of intended use and alternate airports come into play. As mentioned, 14 CFR § 91.103 – Preflight Action is a catchall since the opening paragraph states:

> Each pilot in command shall, before beginning a flight, become familiar with all available information concerning that flight.

14 CFR § 91.103 – Preflight Action has some additional directives, but using NWKRAFT effectively meets the intent of V in enVironment. NWKRAFT is explored in a subsequent chapter.

This brings us to the E in PAVE. E is a reminder to examine any **E**xternal Pressures that might introduce a hazard to the flight. External pressure hazards can be deadly if not mitigated or eliminated in their entirety. According to the FAA's *The PAVE Checklist* which can be found online by typing in *"The PAVE Checklist"* in the search bar, the FAA defines External Pressure as:

> External pressures are influences external to the flight that create a sense of pressure to complete a flight—often at the expense of safety.

From the definition, PICs should objectively assess all influences external to the flight to identify any associated hazards derived from those external influences. *The PAVE Checklist* identifies examples of factors which can be considered external pressures. *The PAVE Checklist* examples are as follows:

- Someone waiting at the airport for the flight's arrival.

- A passenger the pilot does not want to disappoint.
- The desire to demonstrate pilot qualifications.
- The desire to impress someone (Probably the two most dangerous words in aviation are "Watch This!")
- The desire to satisfy a specific personal goal ("get-home-it is," "get-there-it is," and "let's-go-it is")
- The pilot's general goal-completion orientation.
- Emotional pressure associated with acknowledging that skill and experience levels may be lower than a pilot would like them to be. Pride can be a powerful external factor!

It's important to note *The PAVE Checklist* examples are not a complete list. Each PIC is unique and as a result has unique external pressures that may present a hazard. Remember a hazard is a condition or an object that could foreseeably cause or contribute to an incident or aircraft accident. Once the hazard is identified (perceived) as part of the preflight planning, the pilot can assess (process) the predicted severity and likelihood of the potential effect of the external pressure hazard, thus identifying the risk to the flight. Completing the 3P model, the pilot can perform an action to mitigate the risk to the flight. So once again, the pilot has exercised the 3P model as part of the preflight planning phase.

According to *The PAVE Checklist*, management of external pressure is the single most important key to risk management because it is the one risk factor category that can cause a pilot to ignore all the other risk factors. External pressures put time-related pressure on the pilot and figure into a majority of accidents. *The PAVE Checklist* provides examples of ways to manage external pressures, but the key to managing external pressure is to be ready for and accept delays.

To summarize, the PAVE acronym is routinely used as a first step to identify (perceive) hazards associated with each flight. It is a roadmap to explore four independent hazard elements – Pilot, Aircraft, enVironment, and External pressures. Except for external pressures, each of the other hazard elements have subsequent acronyms to help the PIC zero in on specific FAA requirements unique to the Pilot, Aircraft, and enVironment. External pressures are different for each pilot and on each flight and therefore require an objective assessment in every scenario.

Chapter 3: CARE

While PAVE starts the preflight planning process of Perceive, Process, Perform (3P) model by perceiving (or identifying) the hazards associated with four independent hazard elements, CARE assesses which hazards are risks. According to the *Risk Management Handbook* (FAA-H-8083-2A), CARE is risk assessment tool. Broken down, CARE represents **C**onsequences, **A**lternatives, **R**eality, and **E**xternal pressures. Processing (or assessing) the risk of each identified hazard is not so much focused on the FARs, rather CARE gives the PIC a sobering view into assessing the risks associated with identified hazards.

To examine CARE, let's resurrect the example outlined in the pilot section of PAVE. Recall the scenario. A DPE is assessing your ADM skills and knowledge of the relationship between legal and current. The DPE poses a scenario where you are legal to take a friend on a night flight even though your recency of flying at night is over two months ago and your overall night flying experience is barely 5 hours. Assuming you identified the hazard of flying your friend at night with such little experience, how would you process (or assess) the hazard and assess its level of risk associated with the flight?

Starting CARE with **C**onsequences, you might ask yourself, what could go wrong with such a flight? In the extreme, you might consider such a flight has some risk of an accident or fatality, but don't all flights? Flying is inherently risky – right? To a lesser extent, there might be a risk of a hard landing or departure from the runway, but your overall recency of flight is high with about 20 hours over the last 90 days, and you are feeling confident in your abilities. So, after processing the consequences, you recognize that the hazard presents meaningful risk, but you are not ready to scrub the flight yet. CARE then leads you to alternatives.

What are the **A**lternatives or options in processing (or assessing) the hazard associated with this night flight? Remember the goal was to take your visiting friend on a flight, not necessarily a night flight. It was the flying club aircraft availability that slipped you to a night flight option. After exploring an option to trade the flight time to a day flight, you found that to be a dead end. So, for the purposes of this scenario, there are no viable alternatives to reduce the risk associated with the night-flight hazard.

The third piece of processing (or assessing) the hazards in CARE is what is the **R**eality of the situation? In this scenario, the reality is, as a newly minted private pilot, you are looking forward to taking your best friend on a flight who is only in town for a specific time. The circumstances of aircraft availability pushed you into scheduling a night flight and even though you identified the hazard of the situation, you are legal to make the flight. However, a true objective assessment of the situation must include the E in CARE.

The E in CARE is an objective assessment of any **E**xternal Pressures. When you made plans with your best friend to go flying, she indicated she was looking forward to it but did not make any overt signals that she had to go flying. So, in this case the “external pressure” is coming from within. It is rooted in your own desire to take your best friend flying.

In summary, CARE is used to objectively process (or assess) the risks associated with the hazards identified through the PAVE acronym during preflight planning. CARE can also be applied to assess the risks of any hazard recognized on the ground or in flight. Remember, CARE is a risk assessment tool, and its effectiveness depends on using it objectively. We all have our own biases, but taking a moment to assess the risk associated with identified hazards using the questions below will put you on a solid path toward the third 'P' of the 3P model—Perform.

- Consequences – What could go wrong?
- Alternatives – What are the options?
- Reality – What's the situation really like?
- External pressures – Any influencing factors?

Chapter 4: TEAM

The final step of the Perceive, Process, Perform (3P) model is to Perform an action that mitigates the risk associated with any identified hazard. Again, according to Appendix B of the *Risk Management Handbook* (FAA-H-8083-2A), TEAM is a tool which suggests ways to mitigate risk. In short, TEAM represents actions that seek to **T**ransfer, **E**liminate, **A**ccept, or otherwise **M**itigate the risk. Like CARE, TEAM is not focused on the FARs, it is focused on ensuring a safe flight by performing an action to mitigate or eliminate risk associated with identified hazards.

Back to the dilemma of a scheduled night flight with a friend. The perceived hazard is lack of experience of the PIC for the night flight. Notice the hazard was identified as part of the P in PAVE when an objective assessment of the experience (currency) was perceived (identified) to be lacking even if it was legal. Using CARE, risks associated with the hazard were processed (assessed), but now it is time to do something about the risk by using the third P of the 3P model – Perform.

In this scenario, the PIC would like to take his friend flying but knows good Aeronautical Decision Making (ADM) requires him to perform an action to mitigate the risk associated with his lack of night flying recency and experience. Starting down the TEAM ladder, is there a way to **T**ransfer the risk? If the PIC decided to continue with the night flight with his friend, there does not seem to be a way to transfer the risk since the friend is not a pilot. So, he moves on to the next step on the TEAM ladder.

The E in TEAM is a strong one. **E**liminating the risk is the surest way to remove exposure to the hazard. In this case, canceling the night flight eliminates the risk associated with the PIC's inexperience with night flying. While we cannot prove a negative, how many accidents have been prevented by canceling flights with identified hazards where the consequences of flying may have tipped the risk to unacceptable levels? That is why using the CARE acronym is so important. Flying has all sorts of hazards. Perceiving or identifying them using PAVE, then processing or assessing the risk through CARE allows informed decisions to be performed. Canceling a flight where the risk cannot be transferred, accepted, or mitigated is the smart ADM choice. While the E in TEAM comes second, it is important to explore the next 2 methods of "performing" regarding TEAM.

The A in TEAM represents **A**ccepting the risk. Accepting risk should only be done if the acceptance can be done within acceptable safety margins. In this scenario, accepting the risk and flying the night flight without mitigating the risk associated with limited night flying experience seems to be outside the realm of safety margins. That does not mean an accident will occur, only that the hazard of limited night experience could foreseeably cause or contribute to an incident or aircraft accident. Coming to that conclusion and still flying the night flight might be construed as poor ADM. Fortunately, there is the M in TEAM.

M in TEAM stands for **M**itigation. There are ways this PIC might mitigate the risk associated with the hazard of low night flight experience. First, he may ask another pilot or CFI that is current in night flying and has more night flying experience to accompany him and his friend on the flight. His friend would have to ride in back, so it is not ideal but at least he could take his friend flying. The upside of this mitigation plan is both pilots could log PIC time if specific conditions are met[3]. As mentioned, this mitigation plan, while an option is not ideal.

Another mitigation option might be to schedule a night flight before the scheduled flight with the friend. This option mitigates risk associated with the hazard by getting more recent night flight experience. This could be done solo or with another pilot depending on other factors. Performing this action would restart the PAVE process for the flight. Without redoing it here, a subset might be the en**V**ironment for the night flight to gain more recent night currency. If the night is VFR with calm winds and a bright moon, flying the night flight solo might meet acceptable risk margins. However, if it is a dark VFR night with gusty winds, accepting the risk might include mitigating it with another experienced pilot.

Running the 3P model to closure for specific identified hazards during preflight planning ends with TEAM when the Perceived hazard and its Processed risk are addressed by mitigating or eliminating the risk. All the

---

[3] FAA Legal Interpretation (Hicks, 1993) clarifies that in a single-pilot aircraft, a rated pilot may log PIC time as sole manipulator of the controls under 14 CFR § 61.51(e)(1)(i), while another pilot—if designated as the legal PIC—may simultaneously log PIC time under 14 CFR § 61.51(e)(1)(iii), even if not a flight instructor.

perceived hazards and processed risks will still be there if there is no closure through performance to mitigate or eliminate the risk. Remember the 3P model is not just for preflight planning. Perceiving hazards, processing risks, and performing mitigation or elimination of the risk is a constant from preflight through ground operations, flight, and shutdown. Every pilot does this consciously or subconsciously on every flight.

Chapter 5: IMSAFE

The acronym PAVE was introduced as one of the initial acronyms used as part of preflight planning for a flight. As introduced, PAVE represents four independent hazard elements Pilot, Aircraft, enVironment, and External pressures. Beyond the applicable Part 61 FARs regarding regulatory requirements for certification and the currency requirements, pilots should do a self-assessment reinforcing their fitness to fly. The Federal Aviation Administration's (FAA) IMSAFE checklist is a self-assessment tool for pilots to evaluate their fitness to fly. IMSAFE represents the following:

- **I**llness
- **M**edication
- **S**tress
- **A**lcohol
- **F**atigue
- **E**motion

Starting with I for **I**llness, Chapter 8 of the FAA *Aeronautical Information Manual* (AIM) regarding fitness for flight outlines the topic of illness. Paraphrasing chapter 8-1-1 Fitness For Flight, subsection b: even minor illnesses can seriously degrade performance of many piloting tasks vital to safe flight. Therefore, part of an objective self-assessment includes being candid with oneself regarding illness. When considering illness, one should assess not only how they feel and whether they may have impaired judgement, alertness, or limited ability to make routine calculations, but also whether showing up to fly will expose other individuals to a contagious illness. Many of us have gone to work while not feeling well for a variety of reasons (no sick days, project deadline, etc.), but flying is different. The safest option is not to fly while ill.

The M for **M**edication has two parts to consider. The first part is over the counter (OTC) medications that are taken for temporary relief of minor illnesses. The second part is regarding those medications prescribed by a doctor. According to Chapter 8 of the AIM (8-1-1 subsection c 1.) "Pilot performance can be seriously degraded by both prescribed and over-the-counter medications, as well as by the medical conditions for which they are taken". Subsection c 2, further states, "The CFRs prohibit pilots from performing crewmember duties while using any medication that affects the faculties in any way contrary to safety".

In the context of IMSAFE as part of the P in PAVE during preflight planning, Medication should be addressed at the "tactical" level. This assumes, strategically, any prescribed medication has been disclosed and evaluated as part of the periodic medical examination with a designated Aviation Medical Examiner (AME) (the standards for medical certification are contained in 14 CFR part 67). Therefore tactically, M in IMSAFE should focus on any OTC medications and the waiting time for the medication to clear your system.

On the FAA website (faa.gov) under Pilots & Airman, there is a tab for Medical Certification. On the Medical Certification page, select "Aeromedical Safety

Brochures", then select the "Medications and Flying" brochure. In this brochure, the FAA has a "Do not issue" list, outlining information for AMEs when not to issue a medical certificate when an applicant is taking certain medications and a "Do not fly" list of medications and classes/groups of medications pilots should not fly while using without an acceptable wait time after the last dose. The brochure explains and gives examples of the wait time since the last dose. As with anything medical, PICs should always consult a designated AME if there is any doubt or question.

The S in IMSAFE is for **S**tress. Stress is one of those items that is unique for everyone. In the context of the IMSAFE checklist, stress refers to any psychological pressure or emotional strain that could impair a pilot's ability to operate an aircraft safely. This includes both acute stress (such as a recent argument, financial trouble, or work-related tension) and chronic stress (like ongoing health issues or family concerns). Pilots should honestly assess whether stress is affecting their concentration, decision-making, or situational awareness. Students will often be under stress since the "pressure to perform" is inherent in training, however, if stress is significant, it is essential to delay flying until the issue is resolved or manageable, as even subtle distractions can compromise safety in the cockpit. Recognizing and respecting personal limits is a hallmark of sound Aeronautical Decision Making.

The A is for **A**lcohol. The FAA enforces strict rules through 14 CFR § 91.17(a), which states that: No person may act or attempt to act as a crewmember of a civil aircraft–

(4) Within 8 hours after consuming any alcoholic beverage
(5) While under the influence of alcohol
(6) While using any drug that affects the person's faculties in any way contrary to safety
(7) While having an alcohol concentration of 0.04% or greater in a blood or breath specimen

Even small amounts of alcohol can impair judgment, coordination, and reaction time. Residual effects (hangover, fatigue, dehydration) may persist beyond the 8-hour window. PICs must do a self-assessment not just by the clock, but by their actual physical and mental condition. The FAA also encourages pilots to adopt a "bottle to throttle" policy of at least 24 hours, even though the legal minimum is 8 hours. These rules are designed to prevent impairment that could compromise safety.

The next letter of the IMSAFE acronym is F for **F**atigue. Fatigue is insidious in that it can sneak up on a PIC. Often a pilot will not recognize errors made may be rooted in fatigue. Fatigue can be categorized as either acute or chronic. In either case, performance can be degraded. Acute fatigue can be prevented with adequate rest, sleep, exercise, and nutrition. However chronic fatigue is more serious and requires a prolonged period of rest. Pilots need to weigh their fatigue level against the E in PAVE, since External Pressures can push a pilot to fly even when fatigued with catastrophic results. Recall that according to *The PAVE Checklist*, management of external pressure is the single most important key to risk management because it is the one risk factor category that can cause a pilot to ignore all the other risk factors including how fatigued they may be.

This brings the IMSAFE list to E for **E**motion. With all the emphasis on external pressure, when first learning the IMSAFE acronym, many incorrectly associate the E with external pressure, but the FAA encourages pilots to reflect honestly on whether they are emotionally composed and mentally focused enough to safely operate an aircraft. Even if a pilot is physically healthy and well-rested, unresolved emotional distress can lead to distraction or impulsive actions that compromise flight safety. By including "Emotion" in the IMSAFE checklist, the FAA emphasizes that mental and emotional well-being is just as vital as physical health when determining fitness to fly.

To summarize, the IMSAFE acronym gives a PIC the opportunity to objectively do a self-assessment of their fitness to fly. As discussed, it is meant to be used at the "tactical" level during the preflight planning phase. It assumes there are no underlying issues which require a more strategic course of action. As you progress through a flying career, the aspects of IMSAFE will become second nature and as you quickly walk through the acronym, you will be alerted to a physical or mental issue which should trigger you to make good aeronautical decisions so as to not jeopardize safety.

Chapter 6: ARROW

Switching from the P (or Pilot) in PAVE to the A for Aircraft which is the second hazard element of PAVE starts the pilot down the four different acronym paths to ensure the aircraft meets the requirements according to 14 CFR Part 91. The first acronym for the aircraft is ARROW. ARROW represents the following:

- **A**irworthiness Certificate
- **R**egistration Certificate
- **R**adio Station License
- **O**perating Limitations
- **W**eight and Balance

The A in ARROW represents the **A**irworthiness Certificate. There are two aspects to the Airworthiness Certificate. First, according to 14 CFR § 91.203(a)(1) the Airworthiness Certificate must be carried on board the aircraft. Second, according to 14 CFR § 91.203(b) the Airworthiness Certificate must be displayed at the cabin or cockpit entrance so that it is legible to passenger or crew. Therefore, when checking the aircraft paperwork, remember to set the Airworthiness Certificate on top of additional paperwork so it can be seen without having to pull it from its location.

The first R represents **R**egistration Certificate. According to 14 CFR § 91.203(a)(2) the registration certificate must be "effective". Which means it must be current. In January of 2023, there was a change to the duration of effective Aircraft Registration from 3 years to 7 years. This change was codified in 14 CFR § 47.40.

For both the Airworthiness and Registration Certificates, 14 CFR § 91.203(a) is the parent paragraph that dictates the certificates must be "within it" (or on board). Skipping over the parent paragraph in a quick read of the subparagraphs might lead you to believe (incorrectly) they are not required on board.

The second R is for a **R**adio Station License. The Radio Station License is not mandated by the FAA, but rather by the Federal Communications Commission (FCC) and is only required for international flights. The FCC Rule is contained in 47 CFR § 87.18. For many aspiring pilots, this R does not apply and consequently many times the ARROW acronym will be written as AR(R)OW or omit the second R all together.

The O is for **O**perating Limitations. 14 CFR § 91.9(b)(1) and 14 CFR § 21.5 dictate the requirement to carry the Airplane Flight Manual. The Flight Manual must include operating limitations and procedures, as well as performance information necessary for safe operation, as required by the applicable airworthiness standards. The O in ARROW becomes somewhat of a misnomer since often instead of using the O for Operating limitations, many associate the O with POH or the aircraft's Pilot's **O**perating Handbook.

It is worth taking a few paragraphs to get a bit more technical about the O in ARROW. It is important to clarify the difference between Airplane Flight Manual, Pilot's Operating Handbook, and Operating Limitations in general. An Airplane Flight Manual (AFM) is the FAA-approved document specific to an individual aircraft by serial number. It contains legally required information such as operating limitations, procedures, and performance data. The AFM is mandatory for aircraft certified after March 1, 1979, under 14 CFR § 21.5.

The Pilot's Operating Handbook (POH) is a manufacturer-produced manual that often mirrors the AFM content but may include additional helpful information like system descriptions, checklists, and general operating tips. For many modern aircraft, the POH is formatted to meet the General Aviation Manufacturers Association (GAMA) specification and may serve as the AFM if it includes the FAA-required sections and is FAA-approved. In practice, for many general aviation aircraft, especially newer ones, the POH is the AFM—if it is FAA-approved and specific to that aircraft (typically identified by serial number). But not all POHs are AFMs, especially if they are generic or not FAA-approved. So, while AFM and POH are often used interchangeably in casual conversation, only the AFM (or POH if FAA-approved and specific to the aircraft) carries legal weight for regulatory compliance. This brings us to Operating Limitations.

According to 14 CFR § 91.9, the requirement to carry an AFM depends on whether the aircraft is required to have one under 14 CFR § 21.5. An aircraft certified prior to March 1, 1979, is not required to have an AFM, but the requirement to have Operating limitations on board still holds. Therefore, an aircraft not required to have an AFM may satisfy the requirement for Operating limitations by having them placarded in the aircraft. However, an aircraft certified after March 1, 1979, is required to carry an AFM (or POH if it is FAA-approved and specific to the aircraft). This regulatory flexibility helps accommodate legacy aircraft while maintaining safety standards.

Finally, the W in ARROW represents **W**eight and Balance. Weight and Balance is a derived requirement which is not explicitly required under Part 91. However, it is derived from 14 CFR § 91.103 Preflight Action. Since 91.103 directs each PIC before beginning a flight to among other things determine the aircraft's takeoff and landing distance information, a current and specific Weight and Balance of the aircraft must be known.

It is important to understand there are 2 parts of Weight and Balance. First, there is the empty weight of the aircraft. This is done periodically when aircraft equipment is removed, replaced, or upgraded. This provides the baseline for the second part which is the weight and balance applicable to the flight as part of the preflight planning. The first part is required to complete the second part.

In summary, ARROW is a quick acronym to ensure the aircraft has the appropriate certificates, operating limitations, and weight and balance available prior to flight. Furthermore, the documentation provides evidence that safety standards have been met.

Chapter 7: AV1ATES

Continuing with the A in PAVE, AV1ATES is the second of four acronyms used to identify potential hazards associated with the A in PAVE – Aircraft. While ARROW focused on certifications and documentation, AV1ATES focuses on inspections. AV1ATES stands for the following:

- <u>A</u>nnual Inspection
- <u>V</u>OR
- <u>1</u>00-Hour Inspection
- <u>A</u>irworthiness Directives
- <u>T</u>ransponder Inspection
- <u>E</u>LT Inspection
- <u>S</u>tatic System Inspection

Before diving into AV1ATES, it is important to mention not all these inspections are required all the time. Some are required regardless, some are only required if the aircraft will be flown under Instrument Flight Rules (IFR), and the 100-hour inspection is only required if the aircraft is being used "for hire". With that clarification, here is the breakdown.

The first A is for <u>A</u>nnual Inspection. According to 14 CFR § 91.409(a)(1) each aircraft must have an annual inspection by a person authorized by 14 CFR § 43.7. Digging a bit into 14 CFR § 43.7, it identifies 2 types of individuals applicable to this chapter. There is the Airframe and Powerplant (A&P) Mechanic who may approve work they perform within the scope of their certificate and there are the Inspection Authorization (IA) holders who are required for major repairs and alterations, and **annual** inspections. Therefore, the Annual Inspection must be performed by and signed off by an A&P Mechanic with IA.

The V in AV1ATES represents the **V**OR accuracy check. VOR stands for VHF Omnidirectional Range, which is a type of radio navigation system used by aircraft to determine their position and track a course. Like several other items in AV1ATES, the VOR check applies only under specific conditions. Under 14 CFR § 91.171, a VOR accuracy check is required every 30 days only if the pilot intends to use the VOR system for Instrument Flight Rules (IFR) navigation. This requirement is tied to the use of VOR navigation when filed on an IFR flight plan, regardless of weather conditions. If the aircraft will be navigating IFR solely with an approved IFR-certified GPS, the 30-day VOR check is not required. When required, the VOR check can be accomplished in several ways, most commonly by the pilot while airborne.

The 1 in AV1ATES refers to the **1**00-hour inspection. Unlike the annual inspection, the 100-hour inspection can be done and approved by an A&P mechanic, if they hold a valid mechanic certificate issued under 14 CFR Part 65. Also, unlike the annual inspection, 100-hour inspection is only required for those aircraft used "for hire". So, if the aircraft is used for flight training, as a rental, or carries passengers for compensation or hire, the aircraft requires a 100-hour inspection. 14 CFR § 91.409(b) specifies the 100-hour inspection requirement which gives little leeway to overfly the 100-hour inspection, but that leeway is available only to fly to a location where the next 100-hour inspection can be performed, but then that overflown time gets deducted from the next 100-hour inspection to prevent routinely overflying the 100-hour interval.

The second A in AV1ATES represents **A**irworthiness Directives. Airworthiness Directives are issued by the FAA under 14 CFR Part 39 to correct unsafe conditions in aircraft, engines, propellers, or appliances. They are legally enforceable and follow a structured process based on the severity and urgency of the issue. As mentioned in the ARROW chapter, the Airworthiness Certificate does not expire; however, the aircraft is not considered airworthy — and may not be legally operated — unless all applicable Airworthiness Directives have been complied with. Evidence of compliance must be annotated in the aircraft maintenance logbook.

Regulatory information on Airworthiness Directives is contained in 14 CFR § 39, however a definition of the types of Airworthiness Directives can be found on the FAA website at a link on the aircraft certification section. The Airworthiness Directive types (and process) are as follows:

- Standard Airworthiness Directive process is to issue a Notice of Proposed Rule Making (NPRM), followed by a Final Rule – After an unsafe condition is discovered, a proposed solution is published as an NPRM, which solicits public comment on the proposed action. After the comment period closes, the final rule is prepared, taking into account all substantive comments received, with the rule perhaps being changed as warranted by the comments.

- Final Rule; Request for Comments. In certain cases, the critical nature of an unsafe condition may warrant the immediate adoption of a rule without prior notice and solicitation of comments. This is an exception to the standard process. If time by which the terminating action must be accomplished is too short to allow for public comment (that is, less than 60 days), then a finding of impracticability is justified for the terminating action, and it can be issued as an immediately adopted rule. The immediately adopted rule will be published in the Federal Register with a request for comments. The Final Rule AD may be changed later if substantive comments are received.
- Emergency Airworthiness Directives are issued when an unsafe condition exists that requires immediate action by an owner/operator. The intent of an Emergency Airworthiness Directive is to rapidly correct an urgent safety of flight situation.

The T in AV1ATES represents **T**ransponder. The transponder is an electronic device on board the aircraft which responds to interrogation signals from ground-based radar systems. When a radar signal from Air Traffic Control (ATC) hits the aircraft, the transponder automatically replies with coded information. This reply includes:

- A four-digit squawk code assigned by ATC under IFR
- Altitude information (if Mode C or Mode S equipped)
- Aircraft identification (in Mode S transponders)

Transponders must be inspected and tested every 24 calendar months under 14 CFR § 91.413 and they are required in specific airspace in accordance with 14 CFR § 91.215. There is a nuance regarding the inspection requirement since transponders are not required in all airspace when flying under VFR. However, *using* the transponder to squawk 1200 (VFR) triggers the inspection requirement, regardless of whether it is required for that specific flight.

The E in AV1ATES stands for the **E**mergency Locator Transmitter or **E**LT. The ELT is a radio beacon installed in aircraft that transmits a distress signal to aid in locating the aircraft in the event of an accident. The E in AV1ATES assumes the installation of the ELT meets all parts of 14 CFR § 91.207 for placement in the aircraft. However, there are two parts of § 91.207 to draw attention to – battery and inspection. 14 CFR § 91.207(c) specifies ELT batteries must be replaced (or recharged, if the batteries are rechargeable), (1) when the transmitter has been in use for more than 1 cumulative hour or, (2) when 50 percent of their useful life (or, for rechargeable batteries, 50 percent of their useful life of charge) has expired. Regarding inspections per § 91.207(d) each ELT must be inspected within 12 calendar months after the last inspection for:

(1) Proper Installation
(2) Battery corrosion
(3) Operation of the controls and crash sensor
(4) The presence of a sufficient signal radiated from its antenna

Finally, the S in AV1ATES represents the <u>S</u>tatic System. The static system inspection is mandated by 14 CFR § 91.411 Altimeter system and altitude reporting equipment tests and inspections. 14 CFR § 91.411(a)(1) specifically dictates an inspection of each static pressure system, each altimeter instrument, and each automatic pressure altitude reporting system within the preceding 24 calendar months. Like the transponder, Static System inspection is required for IFR flights. Therefore, you must comply with §91.411 and have the static system inspected every 24 calendar months. However, for VFR Flights, you are not required to comply with §91.411, even though the static system feeds critical instruments like the altimeter, airspeed indicator, and vertical speed indicator. That said, the system must still be functionally airworthy under general maintenance rules (e.g.,14 CFR §91.7 and 14 CFR §91.403), even if not formally inspected under 14 CFR § 91.411.

To summarize, AV1ATES is the second acronym stemming from the A (Aircraft) in PAVE. It serves to identify potential hazards of not meeting the FAA mandated inspections required for the aircraft. Walking through the acronym, the source of the inspection requirement was identified and there was discussion on the applicability to IFR, VFR, and whether the aircraft is used for hire.

Chapter 8: A TOMATO FLAMES

If there ever was an aviation acronym that was based on rote memory, A TOMATO FLAMES is it. It looks like someone long ago looked at 14 CFR § 91.205(b) and jumbled 13 of the most applicable items and came up with A TOMATO FLAMES. In all seriousness, A TOMATO FLAMES serves an important function. It focuses on the equipment requirements for day VFR flights. The breakdown of A TOMATO FLAMES is as follows:

- **A**irspeed Indicator

- **T**achometer (for each engine)
- **O**il Pressure Gauge for each engine using pressure system
- **M**agnetic direction indicator (compass)
- **A**ltimeter
- **T**emperature gauge for each liquid-cooled engine
- **O**il Temperature gauge for each air-cooled engine

- **F**uel gauge indicating the quantity of fuel in each tank
- **L**anding gear position indicator if the aircraft has a retractable landing gear
- **A**nti-collision light system (only for airplanes certificated after March 11, 1996)
- **M**anifold Pressure gauge for each altitude engine[4]

---

[4] The FAA uses the term "altitude engine" to mean an engine that is supercharged or turbocharged — i.e., one designed to maintain

- Emergency Locator Transmitter (if required by 14 CFR § 91.207)
- Safety Belts

14 CFR § 91.205(b) has a few caveats so, when referencing the subsections of 14 CFR § 91.205(b) there are paragraphs (1) through (17). However, paragraph (12) references the need for approved flotation gear if the aircraft is operated for hire and beyond power-off gliding distance from shore, paragraph (13) and (14) reference seatbelts and shoulder harnesses so combined they equal the seatbelt requirement, paragraph (16) is "reserved" and paragraph (17) has details on shoulder harnesses for rotorcraft leaving the 13 items listed above as a good representation of the required equipment for day VFR flight.

---

power at higher altitudes. These engines require a manifold pressure gauge because power output is directly related to the pressure in the intake manifold, which varies with throttle, boost, and altitude. Manifold pressure gauges are commonly associated with constant-speed propeller aircraft, because pilots use manifold pressure (instead of RPM alone) to set power. The regulation doesn't tie the requirement to propeller type — it ties it to whether the engine is an "altitude engine." PRACTICAL EXAMPLE: 1) Cessna 172 (fixed-pitch, normally aspirated): No manifold pressure gauge required — just tachometer and fuel/oil instruments; 2) Any turbocharged engine—regardless of propeller type—requires a manifold pressure gauge; 3) Beechcraft Bonanza (constant-speed, normally aspirated): Has a manifold pressure gauge because it's used with the prop governor to set power, but technically 14 CFR § 91.205(b) requires it only if the engine is an "altitude engine." In this case, the manifold pressure gauge is required by the type design, it must be installed and operable under §91.7 (airworthiness) and §91.213 (inoperative instruments).

Since I personally struggled with A TOMATO FLAMES, I am going to take a different approach in relating the acronym back to the A in PAVE by introducing the mnemonic SEA-463. Remember, the purpose behind the CFR is to reduce the risk associated with flying. In PAVE, the FAA draws attention to various sources of hazards (Pilot, Aircraft, enVironment, and External pressure). A TOMATO FLAMES is the traditional acronym associated with the A in PAVE. However, by using SEA-463, we can see more clearly why the FAA has this equipment list. If we take SEA and break it down into **S**afety, **E**ngine, and **A**viate—and add the number of items associated with each—it presents a logical way of remembering the 13 items required for day VFR flight.

Starting with **S**afety. There are 4 equipment items associated with safety.

1. Safety Belts
2. Anti-collision lighting system (only for airplanes certificated after March 11, 1996)
3. Emergency Locator Transmitter
4. Landing Gear position indicator if the aircraft has a retractable landing gear

Followed by **E**ngine. There are 6 equipment items associated with the engine.

1. Oil Pressure Gauge for each engine using pressure system
2. Oil Temperature gauge for each air-cooled engine
3. Tachometer (for each engine)

4. Fuel gauge indicating the quantity of fuel in each tank
5. Temperature gauge for each liquid-cooled engine
6. Manifold Pressure gauge for each altitude engine

And finally **A**viate. There are 3 required items required to safely aviate.

1. Airspeed Indicator
2. Altimeter
3. Magnetic direction indicator (compass)

When considering aircraft equipment, thinking of A TOMATO FLAMES in terms of Safety, Engine, and Aviate (SEA) breaks it down into a manageable and relevant list of items to summarize 14 CFR § 91.205(b). Associating each item with a relevant category elevates A TOMATO FLAMES from rote memory to understanding. By understanding the why behind the list, it is an easy transition to the application and correlation of the required equipment for day VFR flying.

Chapter 9: FLAPS

The fourth and final acronym associated with aircraft representing the A in PAVE is FLAPS. Like A TOMATO FLAMES, FLAPS focuses on required aircraft equipment. Under 14 CFR § 91.205, Powered civil aircraft with standard category U.S. airworthiness certificates: Instrument and equipment requirements, subsection (c) lists the additional equipment required for night VFR. Unlike A TOMATO FLAMES, at least FLAPS sounds associated with flying. FLAPS breaks down as follows:

- **F**uses & spares
- **L**anding light (if for hire)
- **A**nti-collision lights
- **P**osition lights
- **S**ource of electricity adequate for all installed electrical and radio equipment

When arriving at FLAPS to check equipment for night VFR, a couple of things come to mind. First, all equipment required for day VFR also applies to night VFR. Next, this is a good point to explore the different categories of "night" and how they apply not only to night VFR equipment requirements, but also to logging night flight time and night landings for currency requirements. As with most things related to flying it is important to be precise regarding the context of the topic at hand.

Starting with the definition of night in 14 CFR §1.1 General Definitions, "Night means the time between the end of evening civil twilight and the beginning of morning civil twilight, as published in *The Air Almanac*[5], converted to local time." This definition is applicable to when a pilot can log night time. Since we generally don't carry around *The Air Almanac*, many pilots rely on apps to calculate night time. Also, depending on the local latitude, you may come up with a rule of thumb in your area. For example, 30 minutes after sunset or before sunrise works well in mid-latitudes (like the continental U.S.), but the duration varies with latitude and season. So, it is best to establish a baseline for your local area before relying on the 30-minute rule of thumb.

The next reference to night is when is it legal to log a night landing? According to 14 CFR §61.57(b)(1) Night Takeoff and landing experience. The relevant reference is:

> ...no person may act as pilot in command of an aircraft carrying passengers during the period beginning 1 hour after sunset and ending 1 hour before sunrise, unless within the preceding 90 days that person has made at least three take-offs and three landings to a full stop during the period beginning 1 hour after sunset and ending 1 hour before sunrise...

---

[5] *The Air Almanac* is available online in PDF format, free of charge. It is published by the U.S. Naval Observatory (USNO) and can be downloaded directly from their website.

Note, the reference focuses on carrying passengers and the time frame for the take-offs and landings. This does not preclude a pilot from flying solo to regain currency.

This brings us back to FLAPS and its applicability to night VFR equipment requirements. The title of 14 CFR § 91.205(c) is Visual flight rules (night). Nowhere in 14 CFR § 91.205(c) does it mention sunrise to sunset, however that is when the equipment required by the acronym FLAPS applies. This is due to 14 CFR § 91.209 Aircraft Lights. Where the relevant part of 14 CFR § 91.209 states: No person may:

> (a) During the period from sunset to sunrise…
> (1) Operate an aircraft unless it has lighted position lights

So, while 14 CFR § 91.205(c) lists the equipment, the actual applicability windows come from 14 CFR § 91.209 (sunset to sunrise for lights) and §1.1 (civil twilight for logging). Since the applicability starts with lights, all the other equipment is also required from sunset to sunrise.

Beginning with F for **F**uses & spares, 14 CFR § 91.205(c)(6) requires one spare set of fuses, or three spare fuses of each kind required, that are accessible to the pilot in flight. Now might be a good time to mention why the FAA still requires spare fuses. According to FAA's General Aviation and Part 135 Activity Survey, there are about 200,000 active general aviation aircraft in the U.S. fleet. A large portion of these are legacy aircraft designed and certificated decades before 1996. In fact, industry analysts estimate that more than half of the piston-powered GA fleet is made up of aircraft certificated before 1996. Many pre-1965 aircraft still have fuse panels unless owners retrofit breakers during avionics upgrades. Therefore, fuses & spares are still applicable.

Let's cover the L, and A of FLAPS in a single paragraph. The L for **L**anding light is straightforward. 14 CFR § 91.205(c)(4) states, if the aircraft is operated for hire, one electric landing light is required. The A for **A**nti-collision lights is also straightforward in that it is required for all aircraft at night; however, it is worth noting the difference between this reference and the day VFR requirement for an Anti-collision light. Newer aircraft certificated after March 11, 1996, must have anti-collision lights for both day and night operations. For older aircraft, certificated before March 11, 1996, anti-collision lights are not required for day VFR under 14 CFR §91.205(b).

The P of FLAPS represents the **P**osition lights. Position lights show the aircraft's orientation and direction of travel to other pilots. Position lights are the combination of a red light on the left wingtip, green light on the right wingtip, and white light on the tail. In other words, position lights tell others where you are and where you're going while anti-collision lights make sure you are seen at all. Both systems work together to prevent midair conflicts, but they serve distinct roles under 14 CFR Part 91.

Finally, the S of FLAPS represents a **S**ource of electrical energy for all installed electrical and radio equipment. But what does "an adequate source of electrical energy" mean? It means the aircraft must have a reliable system to power all installed electrical and radio equipment during night operations. In practice, this refers primarily to the engine-driven alternator or generator as the continuous source, with the battery serving as a backup. The regulation does not limit the requirement to the battery alone; instead, it ensures that the aircraft has sufficient electrical capacity to operate essential lights, instruments, and radios safely throughout the flight.

This chapter unpacked a lot of information beyond just the night equipment requirements. It summarized the different context for "night" applicable to logging night flight time, specific requirements for night landing currency, and of course the applicability of FLAPS in identifying required aircraft equipment for night VFR flying.

Chapter 10: NWKRAFT

NWKRAFT is another acronym that seems to focus on rote memory. Again, someone a long time ago looked at 14 CFR § 91.103 and picked out the items to make up NWKRAFT. All pilots should be familiar with 14 CFR § 91.103 since this reference is a "catch all" placing responsibility on the PIC to "...before beginning a flight, become familiar with all available information concerning that flight". Fortunately, it has a "must include" list of items that make up NWKRAFT. NWKRAFT breaks down as follows:

- **N**OTAMs – Notice to Airmen[6]
- **W**eather
- **K**nown traffic delays
- **R**unway lengths of intended use
- **A**lternative airports available
- **F**uel requirements
- **T**akeoff and landing distance information

Starting with the N for **N**otice to Airmen. 14 CFR § 91.103 does not mention NOTAM anywhere in the section. However, the FAA considers NOTAMs as part of "all available information" necessary for safe flight. Practically, NOTAMs are safety-critical and contain time-sensitive hazards (e.g., runway closures, navaid outages, airspace restrictions). Therefore, if a pilot fails

[6] Historically: Notice to Airmen (reflecting traditional aviation language). It was temporarily changed to Notice to Air Missions for inclusivity from 2021-2025. In February 2025, FAA reverted back to Notice to Airmen to align with international standards.

to check NOTAMs and encounters a closed runway or restricted airspace, the FAA can cite them under 14 CFR § 91.103. While checking NOTAMs can seem daunting at times, Flight Service and electronic briefing systems automatically include NOTAMs when a pilot requests a preflight briefing. In fact, popular apps include a breakdown of applicable NOTAMs based on route of flight thereby streamlining the process.

The W in NWKRAFT represents a check of the **W**eather. Focusing on weather is an integral part of primary flight training. In December 2024, the FAA published a comprehensive guide to aviation weather, consolidating information from multiple FAA Advisory Circulars (ACs) into one resource the *Aviation Weather Handbook*, FAA-H-8083-28A. This supersedes the 2022 edition and replaces multiple FAA Advisory Circulars[7] (ACs). PICs are required to understand the current and forecast weather conditions that might be applicable to the flight.

The K represents being aware of any **K**nown traffic delays. 14 CFR § 91.103(a) starts out "For a flight under IFR…" and if you were to stop reading there thinking 14 CFR § 91.103(a) doesn't apply to VFR flights, you'd be wrong because the second part of that sentence says "…or a flight not in the vicinity of an airport…". So, the rest of the paragraph applies equally

[7] With the December 2024 publishing of FAA-H-8083-28A, the following ACs were canceled: AC 00-6: Aviation Weather; AC 00-24: Thunderstorms; AC 00-30: Clear Air Turbulence Avoidance; AC 00-45: Aviation Weather Services; AC 00-54: Pilot Windshear Guide; AC 00-57: Hazardous Mountain Winds

to VFR flights with the last part of the paragraph stating "…and any known traffic delays of which the pilot in command has been advised by ATC."

But where does the PIC get information regarding traffic delays? Traffic delays are reported to the Flight Service, so when a pilot gets a standard brief through Flight Service (e.g., 1800WXBRIEF.com) before the flight, the briefer should include any known traffic delays as reported by ATC. Electronic flight planning tools also pull information directly from the FAA's National Airspace System (NAS) data feeds, which includes traffic management initiatives (delays, reroutes, restrictions), airport status (closures, capacity limits), weather impacts on the system, NOTAMs and advisories, and real-time operational data. Therefore, while most pilots think "Known traffic delays" applies to IFR flights, they also apply to VFR flights not in the vicinity of the departure airport or in cases where the flight originates and/or terminates at a controlled airport.

Next is the R for **R**unway lengths of intended use. 14 CFR § 91.103(b) specifically calls out "For any flight, runway lengths at airports of intended use…" as part of "all available information" concerning the flight. This is the precursor to final letter T for takeoff and landing data since part of the preparation for a flight includes knowing whether the runway of intended use is appropriate for the conditions applicable to the flight.

Let's tie the A and F in NWKRAFT together in a single paragraph. The A represents **A**lternative airports available while the F represents the **F**uel requirements.

When planning a VFR flight, 14 CFR § 91.151 requires enough fuel to reach the destination and then continue for 30 minutes day VFR (45 minutes night VFR), but 14 CFR § 91.103 adds another layer by requiring the pilot to be familiar with alternatives available if the flight cannot be completed. This means that while an alternate airport is not explicitly mandated under VFR rules, the pilot must still identify suitable alternates during preflight planning and ensure that fuel reserves are sufficient to reach an alternate if a diversion becomes necessary. Therefore, *if you identify an alternate* under 91.103 (because you might not be able to complete the flight to your destination), you must ensure you have enough fuel to reach that alternate and still meet the reserve requirement after arrival at the alternate[8].

The final letter in NWKRAFT is the T for **T**akeoff and landing distance information. Recall back to the W of the ARROW acronym. It called attention to the Weight and Balance of the aircraft, and the need to know both the empty weight and the weight applicable to the pending flight. Computing the weight and balance for the pending flight allows the PIC to reference the Airplane Flight Manual (or approved POH) to derive the specific takeoff and landing data for the conditions. This is a specific requirement of 14 CFR § 91.103(b)(1)

---

[8] VFR pilots are not held to IFR fuel rules, but under 14 CFR § 91.103 they must still plan for reasonable alternatives. Enforcement cases show that running short of fuel after ignoring obvious alternate needs can violate § 91.103 or § 91.13, even though the "destination + alternate + reserve" requirement exists only for IFR (§ 91.167).

and (2). Paragraph 2 emphasizes the need to consider "expected values of airport elevation and runway slope, aircraft gross weight, and wind and temperature" in the takeoff and landing calculations.

The NWKRAFT acronym is an important "catch-all." It highlights the responsibility under 14 CFR § 91.103 for the PIC to "become familiar with all available information concerning that flight". Understanding the specific items and reviewing each item (as applicable) to the flight planning should put the PIC on track to meet the flight planning obligations. However, each flight is unique, and pilots should pause to ensure they have considered "all available information" even if it is outside of what NWKRAFT represents.

Chapter 11: DECIDE

The final acronym to explore in this book is the DECIDE model. While Advisory Circular 60-22 *Aeronautical Decision Making* (1991) codifies the DECIDE model, it was not its original source. The FAA first introduced DECIDE in 1987 through *Aeronautical Decision Making for Instrument Pilots* (DOT/FAA/PM-86/43). In the forward to that document, the FAA notes it was the product of "ten years of research, development, testing and evaluation of the effectiveness of teaching judgment and decision making." As its acronym suggests, the DECIDE model provides a simple way to remember the key elements of the decision-making process. The DECIDE model is represented as follows:

- **D**etect
- **E**stimate
- **C**hoose
- **I**dentify
- **D**o
- **E**valuate

It is important to note the DECIDE model is a continuous loop starting with the first D for **D**etect. In your scan, you detect a change has occurred. The change is likely unexpected. As an example, flying on final leg of a cross country where you planned for a ground speed of 90 knots (kts), you detect your ground speed is closer to 60 kts due to a stiff headwind. For ease of math, assume the leg was 90 Nautical Miles (NM) and you planned for an hour of fuel on the leg.

The next step in the model is E for **E**stimate. This is where you determine whether the change you detected requires corrective action. In our example, you now know it will take an hour and a half (1+30) to complete the leg. You had planned to arrive with +45 minutes of fuel, but with the slower ground speed you now estimate only +15 minutes of fuel on arrival. Since 14 CFR § 91.151 requires enough fuel to reach your destination and then continue for at least +30 minutes under day VFR, this estimate makes it clear you must respond to the change you detected.

This brings us to the C for **C**hoose. After detecting the change and estimating its impact, you must now choose the best course of action to maintain safety and compliance. In this example, your estimate shows that continuing as planned would leave you with only +15 minutes of fuel upon arrival, which is below the legal minimum required by regulation and more importantly it leaves you with the possibility of running out of fuel short of your destination. Faced with this situation, you must choose from among several possible actions. You might divert to a nearby airport to refuel, adjust your route to minimize the headwind (if possible), or even decide to terminate the flight early. The key in the Choose step is to evaluate the available alternatives and select the option that best mitigates the risk while ensuring you remain within both regulatory requirements and safe operating margins.

The next step in the model is I for **I**dentify. Once you have chosen a course of action, you must identify the steps needed to carry it out. In our example, you decided that continuing to the destination without refueling would leave you below the legal minimum fuel reserve and more importantly it leaves you with the possibility of running out of fuel short of your destination. Therefore, you identify the specific actions required to mitigate the risk. That might include locating the nearest suitable airport along your route, checking its fuel availability, reviewing VFR pattern procedures, and contacting Flight Service to update your flight plan with the diversion. The identify step is about breaking down your chosen option into clear, actionable tasks that will move you toward a safe outcome.

The next step in the model is D for **D**o. After identifying the specific actions required, you now carry them out. In our example, you have chosen to divert to a nearby airport to refuel and identified the steps necessary to make that diversion. The Do step is where you execute those actions: you contact Flight Service to amend your flight plan, adjust your navigation to the new course, and prepare for the arrival to the alternate airport. This step emphasizes that decision-making is not complete until you act on the choice you made, turning planning into tangible action that directly addresses the risk you detected.

The final step in the model is E for **E**valuate. After carrying out your chosen action, you must evaluate the results to ensure the risk has been properly mitigated. In our example, you diverted to a nearby airport to refuel and amended your flight plan with Flight Service. Now you evaluate whether the diversion achieved the intended outcome. The Evaluate step is about confirming that your decision solved the problem and determining whether further adjustments are needed. If the situation has changed again, the DECIDE model loops back to Detect, reminding you that decision-making in aviation is a continuous process of monitoring, assessing, and adapting.

In summary, the DECIDE model is an effective framework within the decision-making process to reduce risk in flight operations. It begins with the deliberate detection of a change that requires action to maintain safety. While the FAA has codified the model into structured steps, many of the decisions we make throughout the day naturally follow its logic. The key is to maintain a vigilant scan that identifies unexpected changes, allowing you to work through the model systematically to mitigate risk and achieve a safe outcome.

Conclusion

The journey from aspiring pilot to confident aviator is built not only on technical skill but also on the ability to make sound decisions in dynamic environments. Acronyms, while simple in form, serve as powerful tools to anchor complex concepts in memory and practice. By exploring each acronym in context—whether through the proactive 3P model, the structured DECIDE process, or supporting frameworks like PAVE, CARE, TEAM, and IMSAFE—this book has shown how they interconnect to strengthen Aeronautical Decision Making and Risk Management, the very heart of Single-Pilot Resource Management.

What may first appear overwhelming becomes manageable when acronyms are understood as more than checklists; they are bridges linking regulations, guidance, and practical application in the cockpit. Each acronym provides a lens through which pilots can perceive hazards, process the associated risks, and perform actions that lead to safer outcomes. In doing so, they transform rote memorization into meaningful correlation, ensuring that decisions are deliberate, resources are managed effectively, and risks are mitigated before they lead to unsafe outcomes.

Ultimately, the consistent use of these acronyms fosters a mindset of vigilance, adaptability, and professionalism. They remind us that safe flight is not the result of chance but of disciplined preparation and thoughtful execution. As you continue your journey in aviation, let these acronyms serve not as isolated memory aids, but as integrated tools that guide your judgment, sharpen your awareness, and reinforce your commitment to safety. In mastering them, you not only meet the standards of the FAA—you embody the principles of a pilot in command.

Glossary

3P – Perceive, Process, Perform – A risk-management model in aeronautical decision making that guides pilots through three steps: Perceive hazards, Process the associated risks, and Perform risk-mitigation actions.

A TOMATO FLAMES – A mnemonic used by pilots to remember the required instruments and equipment for VFR flight in powered aircraft under 14 CFR § 91.205(b).

AC – Advisory Circulars are FAA guidance documents that explain regulations, recommend procedures, and provide educational information. They are non-binding but widely used to promote safe and standardized aviation practices.

ACS - Airman Certification Standards are FAA documents that outline the knowledge, risk management, and skill requirements for pilot certification. They replaced the Practical Test Standards (PTS) and ensure pilots are evaluated on both technical proficiency and safe decision-making.

ADM – Aeronautical Decision-Making. The FAA's systematic approach to pilot decision-making. It involves perceiving hazards, assessing risks, and performing actions to ensure safe outcomes. ADM integrates risk management tools and human-factor awareness to reduce accidents and improve flight safety.

AIM – Aeronautical Information Manual. The FAA's primary guide to flight information and air traffic control procedures. It provides non-regulatory guidance on safe and compliant operations in the National Airspace System.

ARROW – The mnemonic for required aircraft documents. It stands for Airworthiness Certificate, Registration Certificate, Radio Station License (international flights only), Operating Limitations, and Weight & Balance data.

AV1ATES – The mnemonic for required aircraft inspections and maintenance. Stands for Annual, VOR, 100-hour, Airworthiness Directives, Transponder, ELT, and Static system checks.

CARE – Consequences, Alternatives, Reality, External pressures. The FAA risk management tool used in the "Process" step of the 3P model. It guides pilots to evaluate hazards by considering consequences, alternatives, reality, and external pressures before making a decision.

CFI – Certificated Flight Instructor. An FAA-certificated pilot authorized to provide flight instruction, endorse students for tests, and ensure training meets FAA standards.

CFIT – Controlled Flight Into Terrain. An accident where a fully functional aircraft, under pilot control, is unintentionally flown into terrain, water, or obstacles due to loss of situational awareness.

CFR – Code of Federal Regulations. The official collection of U.S. federal rules. In aviation, Title 14 CFR contains the FAA's Federal Aviation Regulations (FARs), which govern pilot certification, aircraft maintenance, and flight operations.

DECIDE – Detect, Estimate, Choose, Identify, Do, Evaluate. An FAA decision-making framework which guides pilots through a structured process to recognize problems, select actions, and assess outcomes.

Dual Time Given – Flight time logged by a Certificated Flight Instructor (CFI) when providing instruction to a student or certificated pilot. This entry documents the instructor's teaching activity and is used to track instructional experience, endorsements, and compliance with FAA requirements for maintaining instructor privileges.

Dual Time Received – Flight time logged by a student or certificated pilot when receiving instruction from a CFI. This entry records the pilot's training experience toward certificates, ratings, endorsements, or currency requirements. If the pilot is already certificated and is the sole manipulator of the controls in an aircraft for which they are rated, they may log this time as both Dual Received and PIC (Pilot in Command) simultaneously.

eCFR - Electronic Code of Federal Regulations. Online, continuously updated version of the CFR. Provides the most current FAA regulations under Title 14, used by pilots and aviation professionals for compliance and reference.

FAA – Federal Aviation Administration. U.S. government agency under the Department of Transportation that regulates civil aviation, certifies pilots and aircraft, manages air traffic control, and ensures safety in the National Airspace System.

FAASTeam – Federal Aviation Administration Safety Team. FAA's outreach program to reduce aviation accidents. Provides training, seminars, and partnerships to promote safety culture, especially in general aviation.

FAR – Federal Aviation Regulations. Rules in Title 14 CFR issued by the FAA that govern civil aviation in the U.S., including pilot certification, aircraft maintenance, and flight operations.

FCC – Federal Communications Commission. U.S. government agency regulating communications. In aviation, it licenses aircraft radios and requires radio station licenses for international flights.

FLAPS – The mnemonic for required night VFR equipment. Stands for Fuses, Landing light (for hire), Anti-collision lights, Position lights, and Source of electrical power.

GAMA – General Aviation Manufacturers Association. International trade association representing general aviation manufacturers of aircraft, engines, avionics, and components. Founded in 1970, GAMA promotes aviation safety, industry growth, and public understanding of general aviation's role worldwide.

IMSAFE – The FAA mnemonic for pilot self-assessment. Stands for Illness, Medication, Stress, Alcohol, Fatigue, and Emotion. Used to evaluate personal fitness before flight.

NOTAM - Notice to Airmen. Information essential to flight operations that is time-critical and not known far enough in advance to be published in charts or other operational publications. NOTAMs alert pilots to temporary hazards, changes, or conditions affecting the National Airspace System.

NPRM – Notice of Proposed Rule Making. A public notice published in the Federal Register by agencies like the FAA to propose regulatory changes and invite public comment before issuing a final rule.

NWKRAFT – The mnemonic for preflight planning requirements under 14 CFR § 91.103. It stands for NOTAMs, Weather, Known traffic delays, Runway lengths, Alternatives, Fuel requirements, and Takeoff and landing performance data.

OTC – Over The Counter (medications). Non-prescription drugs available to the public. Pilots must use caution, as many OTC medications (such as antihistamines or cold remedies) can cause drowsiness or impair judgment, making them unsafe for flight.

PAVE – The FAA risk management mnemonic which stands for Pilot, Aircraft, enVironment, and External pressures. It is used to evaluate risks before flight and support safe decision making.

PIC – Pilot in Command. The pilot who has final authority and responsibility for the operation and safety of a flight. PIC time may be logged when a pilot is acting as PIC, the sole manipulator of the controls of an aircraft for which they are rated, or serving as PIC in an aircraft that requires more than one pilot.

SRM – Single-Pilot Resource Management. FAA concept for managing all available resources in single-pilot operations. It includes ADM, risk management, task management, situational awareness, CFIT avoidance, and automation management.

TEAM – The FAA risk management mnemonic which stands for Transfer, Eliminate, Accept, and Mitigate. It is a tool that provides structured options for handling hazards and making safer decisions.

References

Federal Aviation Administration. *Airplane Flying Handbook* (FAA-H-8083-3C). Washington, DC: U.S. Department of Transportation, 2021.

Federal Aviation Administration. *Risk Management Handbook* (FAA-H-8083-2A). Washington, DC: U.S. Department of Transportation, 2022.

Federal Aviation Administration. *Pilot's Handbook of Aeronautical Knowledge* (FAA-H-8083-25C). Washington, DC: U.S. Department of Transportation, 2023.

Federal Aviation Administration. *Aviation Weather Handbook* (FAA-H-8083-28A). Washington, DC: U.S. Department of Transportation, 2024.

Federal Aviation Administration. *Private Pilot for Airplane Category Airman Certification Standards* (FAA-S-ACS-6C). Washington, DC: U.S. Department of Transportation, 2023.

Federal Aviation Administration. *Aeronautical Information Manual*. Washington, DC: U.S. Department of Transportation, current edition.

Federal Aviation Administration. Advisory Circular 60-22 *Aeronautical Decision Making*. Washington, DC: U.S. Department of Transportation, 1991.

Federal Aviation Administration. *Aeronautical Decision Making for Instrument Pilots* (DOT/FAA/PM-86/43). Washington, DC: U.S. Department of Transportation, 1987.

Federal Aviation Administration. *The PAVE Checklist*. Washington, DC: U.S. Department of Transportation, current edition.

U.S. Government Publishing Office. *Code of Federal Regulations, Title 14: Aeronautics and Space*. Washington, DC: U.S. Government Publishing Office, current edition.

www.ingramcontent.com/pod-product-compliance
Lightning Source LLC
LaVergne TN
LVHW021200160826
845679LV00024B/2183

* 9 7 9 8 2 1 8 9 2 6 8 5 4 *